LIFE IS SHORT,
PRAY HARD

Mary Compton and David Compton

LIFE IS SHORT, PRAY HARD

FORBIDDEN FRUIT II

More Roadside Church Signs Across America

NEW AMERICAN LIBRARY

NEW AMERICAN LIBRARY
Published by New American Library, a division of
Penguin Putnam Inc., 375 Hudson Street, New York, New York 10014, U.S.A.
Penguin Books Ltd, 80 Strand, London WC2R 0RL, England
Penguin Books Australia Ltd, 250 Camberwell Road, Camberwell, Victoria 3124, Australia
Penguin Books Canada Ltd, 10 Alcorn Avenue, Toronto, Ontario, Canada M4V 3B2
Penguin Books (N.Z.) Ltd, Cnr Rosedale and Airborne Roads, Albany, Auckland 1310, New Zealand

Penguin Books Ltd, Registered Offices: Harmondsworth, Middlesex, England

First published by New American Library, a division of Penguin Putnam Inc.

First Printing, March 2003
1 3 5 7 9 10 8 6 4 2

REGISTERED TRADEMARK—MARCA REGISTRADA

LIBRARY OF CONGRESS CATALOGING-IN-PUBLICATION DATA:

Compton, Mary Katherine.
Life is short, pray hard : forbidden fruit II : more roadside church signs across America /
Mary Compton and David Compton.
p.   cm.
ISBN 0-451-20783-1 (alk. paper)
1. Church signs—United States—Humor.   2. American wit and humor.   I. Compton, David.   II. Title.
BV653.7.C67 2003
254'.4—dc21   2002031530

Printed in the United States of America

BOOKS ARE AVAILABLE AT QUANTITY DISCOUNTS WHEN USED TO PROMOTE PRODUCTS OR SERVICES. FOR INFORMATION PLEASE WRITE TO PREMIUM MARKETING DIVISION, PENGUIN PUTNAM INC., 375 HUDSON STREET, NEW YORK, NEW YORK 10014.

In memory of the Reverend Paul H. Pittman III,
who followed the signs and found his way to heaven.

Introduction

It's surprising how fast our notebook filled up again since we compiled *Forbidden Fruit Creates Many Jams*, our first volume of roadside church signs. Originally, we thought we had discovered the large majority of these witty and thought-provoking messages. Surely the several hundred of these "sentence sermons" contained in the pages of our little publication represented just about all there was.

We were so wrong.

Churches from which we had collected our first messages were now posting signs we had never seen. We found new churches, new maxims and admonitions begging to be written down. Friends and family and total strangers sent even more. We soon had compiled an all-new list, every bit as humorous and profound as the first.

The messages in this second volume have many things in common with those in *Forbidden Fruit Creates Many Jams*. They are, as a group, an extremely simple, effective way of communicating with passersby. They make you think, then smile. Sometimes it's the other way around.

The title of this book—*Life Is Short, Pray Hard*—is a delightful pun on a well-known sports slogan. We think this is the best kind of roadside church sign: at first glance amusing; then, after reflection, a serious thought to carry with you throughout the day, wherever you are going.

As you turn the page—or turn the corner to see a sign along your own journey—we hope you experience the same delight of unanticipated inspiration.

People do odd things to get even.

◆

Practice makes perfect, so be careful
what you practice.

◆

Remember the rabbit foot didn't work
for the rabbit.

One good thing you can give away and
still keep: Your word.

✦

Daily prayers lessen daily cares.

Small deeds done are better than
great deeds planned.

◆

A half-truth is a whole lie.

◆

If you suppress a moment of anger,
you can prevent a day of sorrow.

LIFE HAS MANY CHOICES—

ETERNITY HAS TWO.

WHAT'S YOURS?

GRACE: God's Riches At Christ's Expense.

◆

We're all invited to a heavenly feast,
but we must RSVP!

Faith is caught, not taught.

✦

Past failures are guideposts for future successes.

MORALITY, LIKE ART, CONSISTS IN DRAWING A LINE SOMEWHERE.

God has subpoenaed all of us as witnesses.

◆

Your life may be the only Bible some folks read.

Laughter is the shortest distance
between two people.

✦

My way is the highway.
—God

✦

Life is like tennis: Serve well and
you seldom lose.

Improve your outlook by looking up.

✦

The converted heart leads to an inverted purse.

SMOKING WON'T SEND YOU TO HELL, IT'LL JUST MAKE YOU SMELL LIKE YOU'VE BEEN THERE.

The heart is an organ; keep it in tune with Jesus.

✦

GOOD without GOD becomes O.

God may break us in order to remake us.

♦

God's mercy is greater than your greatest sin.

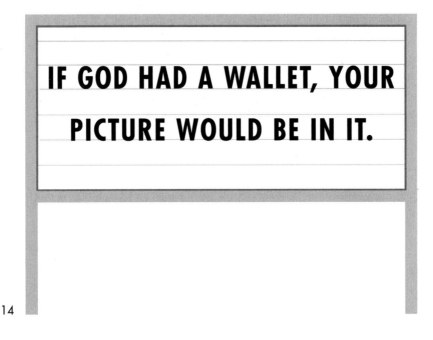

IF GOD HAD A WALLET, YOUR PICTURE WOULD BE IN IT.

14

Atheism is a non-prophet organization.

✦

God sends away empty those full of themselves.

✦

This is just a little country church with a
lost and found.

HE WHO IS ALWAYS
BLOWING A FUSE IS
USUALLY IN THE DARK.

A bad conscience has a very good memory.

◆

Courage is not absence of fear,
but mastery over it.

18

A hypocrite is a person who's not
himself on Sunday.

✦

Opportunity knocks once. Temptation leans
on the doorbell!

✦

If you're far from God in life, you'll be
far from God in death.

Heavenly forecast . . . Reign forever!

✦

Things that are not eternal are already out of date.

✦

I don't know what the future holds,
but I know who holds the future.

Success has made failures of many people.

✦

I may not be who I want to be, but I thank God
I am not who I was.

✦

O God, take me, break me, make me.

EVEN A FISH STAYS OUT OF TROUBLE IF HE KEEPS HIS MOUTH SHUT.

It is wise to walk with someone who knows the way.

◆

God's Word brings peace in the presence of pain.

◆

The greatest man in history was also the poorest.

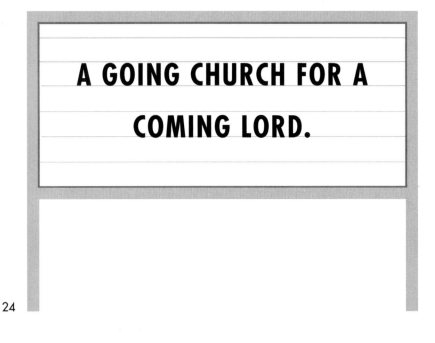

24

If you feel far away from God, who moved?

◆

Get rich quick! Count your blessings!

What we weave in this world we will wear in heaven.

◆

Happiness can be thought, taught, and caught, but not bought.

◆

Most gossips get caught in their own mouthtraps.

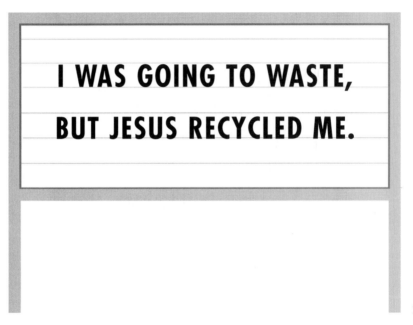

I intend to live forever—so far, so good.

◆

When you bury the hatchet,
don't mark the grave.

◆

A smile is a curve that sets a lot of things straight.

Confessing your sins is no substitute
for forsaking them.

✦

The trouble with self-made people is they
worship their creator.

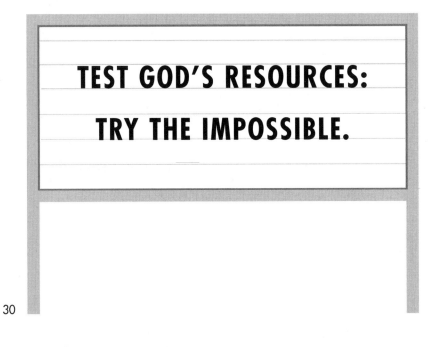

TEST GOD'S RESOURCES:

TRY THE IMPOSSIBLE.

30

Faith in Jesus is the believer's passport to heaven.

✦

When growth stops, decay begins.

God is dead.
—Nietzsche
Nietzsche is dead.
—God

✦

Why don't you stop trying to figure God out
and start trying to figure Him in?

Swallowing your pride seldom
leads to indigestion.

✦

A friendship is a treasure beyond measure.

To make a mountain out of a molehill,
just add dirt.

Jesus is an equal opportunity Savior.

◆

Is God your steering wheel or your spare tire?

Reading the Bible without meditating on it is like eating without chewing.

✦

A day hemmed with prayer seldom unravels.

Without the Son, there would be total
darkness in the world.

◆

Faith honors God, and God honors faith.

◆

Of the body's muscles, the hardest to keep
in shape is the heart.

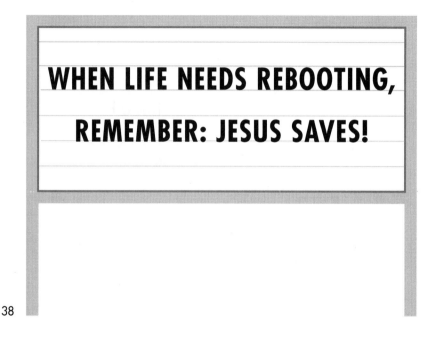

38

Giving is sowing, and God promises a harvest!

✦

Christianity is a pilgrimage,
not a sightseeing tour.

TODAY IS A GIFT FROM GOD.

THAT'S WHY IT'S CALLED

"THE PRESENT."

Pray for a good harvest, but continue to hoe.

✦

All that's necessary for evil to win is for good
people to do nothing.

The curvature of the moral spine is a disease
that only the Great Physician can cure.

✦

Is your faith ancient history or current events?

Salvation is what we receive,
not what we achieve.

◆

What we sow in time, we reap in eternity.

Are you living or existing?

✦

Most people want to serve God—but only
in an advisory capacity.

✦

Live life prepared to die, and die
prepared to live.

A shortcut is often a temptation in disguise.

◆

If you don't have anything to pray about,
thank God you don't.

◆

P.U.S.H.—Pray Until Something Happens.

Faith is bread for daily use, not cake
for special occasions.

✦

The best exercise is stooping down and
lifting up another.

✦

Growing old is mandatory;
growing up is optional.

The world uses duct tape to fix everything.
Jesus used nails.

✦

May all your troubles be as short as your
New Year's resolutions.

✦

Honk if you love peace and quiet.

THE CLOSEST DISTANCE BETWEEN A PROBLEM AND ITS SOLUTION IS THE DISTANCE BETWEEN YOUR KNEES AND THE FLOOR.

50

An oasis of faith at a busy crossroads.

✦

If you're not ready to forgive, you're not ready.

Sin would have fewer partakers if the consequences occurred immediately.

✦

Good example has twice the value of good advice.

Kindness: difficult to give away,
it usually comes back.

✦

Part-time faith, like part-time jobs,
cannot fully support you.

The empty tomb proves Christianity.
The empty church denies it.

✦

Man's way leads to a hopeless end!
God's way leads to an endless hope!

Write your plans in pencil but give
God the eraser.

◆

Worry ends where faith begins.

You can preach a better sermon with your life than with your lips.

✦

Cultivate good habits. The bad ones all grow wild.

✦

Feed on the Bread of Life, then serve it to others.

GODISNOWHERE
(now read it again)

✦

The largest room in the world is the room
for self-improvement.

✦

Life makes some people better and others bitter.

If you brood over your troubles, you hatch despair.

✦

Christ believed is salvation received.

✦

To belittle is to be little.

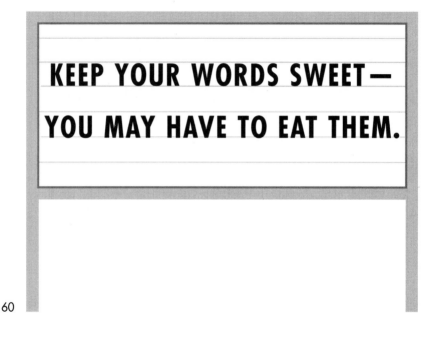

KEEP YOUR WORDS SWEET—
YOU MAY HAVE TO EAT THEM.

You can give without loving but you cannot
love without giving.

✦

☀ Be the soul provider for your children.

Who wants to be a Christianaire?

◆

In the sentence of life the Devil may be a comma, but do not let him be the period!

◆

God is more interested in our availability than our ability.

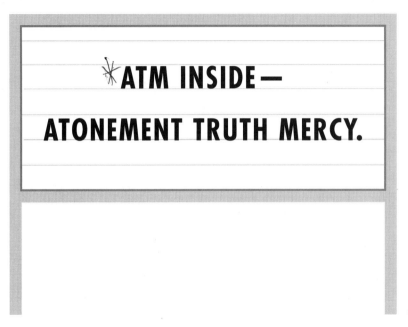

63

If you worry, why pray? If you pray, why worry?

◆

God is a promise keeper.

◆

Will the road you're on get you to my place?
—God

Have no fear in tomorrow—
Jesus is already there.

✦

Worry is a waste of the imagination.

Salvation—it does a person good.

✦

Men do not fail; they give up trying.

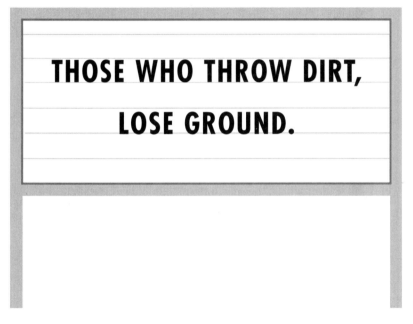

THOSE WHO THROW DIRT,

LOSE GROUND.

Life does not have to be perfect to be wonderful.

✦

The past should be a guidepost,
not a hitching post.

Instead of pointing a finger, hold out a hand.

◆

We are overdressed when wrapped
up in ourselves.

◆

Fall seven times—stand up eight!

Jesus invested his life in you—have you shown any interest?

◆

Human judgment's greatest flaw: it doesn't have all the facts.

◆

When you don't witness, you just did.

Jesus never taught how to preach,
only how to pray.

✦

Adversity introduces you to yourself.

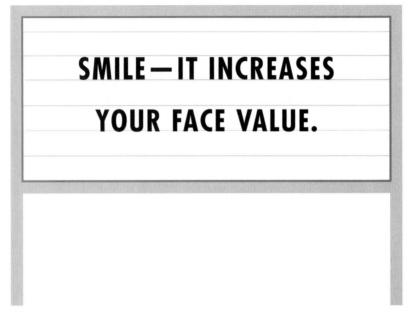

SMILE—IT INCREASES
YOUR FACE VALUE.

If you keep courting trouble,
you will soon be married to it.

♦

Faith is a journey, not a destination.

Any time God closes a door, it's for our protection.
When He opens a door, it's an invitation.

✦

Following the path of least resistance makes
rivers and people crooked.

Life is a puzzle—look here for the missing peace.

◆

The Saints win here every Sunday!

SATAN SUBTRACTS AND DIVIDES. GOD ADDS AND MULTIPLIES.

When life knocks you on your knees, pray there.

✦

God's plans for us are better than our own.

✦

Don't expect a thousand-dollar answer to
a ten-cent prayer.

Sin is a progressive disease—one sin
leads to another.

◆

Some folks won't look up until they are
flat on their backs.

◆

If God is your Father, the church is your mother.

A man's character is like a fence. It cannot be strengthened by whitewash.

◆

God is up to something good.

◆

Prayer is the next best thing to being there.

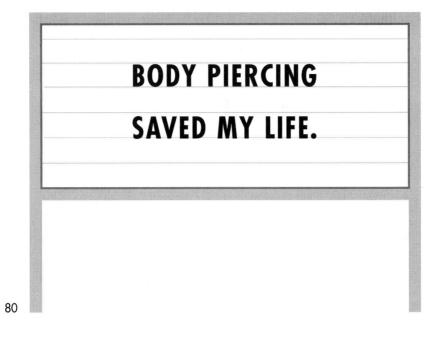

BODY PIERCING

SAVED MY LIFE.

80

The Lord works from the inside out. The world works from the outside in.

✦

If the going gets easy, you may be going downhill.

✦

Holding a grudge is letting someone live rent-free in your head.

WISDOM HAS TWO PARTS:

HAVING A LOT TO SAY

AND NOT SAYING IT.

If you jump to conclusions,
you make terrible landings.

◆

I'd rather be a fool in the eyes of men,
than a fool in the eyes of God.

If you think meek is weak, try being meek for a week.

✦

Patience is trusting in God's timing.

Jesus is right for whatever is wrong in your life.

◆

Jesus never asks us to enter a valley
He has not passed through.

◆

A baby is God's opinion that the world
should go on.

You are in the driver's seat,
but God holds the map.

✦

People are like tea bags—you have to put them in
hot water before you know how strong they are.

We welcome you with open Psalms.

✦

Impatience is a form of unbelief.

✦

Let's meet at my house Sunday before the game.

Wrinkled with burden? Come on into church
for a faith lift!

◆

Creation is a finger pointing to God.

◆

Live so that the preacher doesn't have to
lie at your funeral.

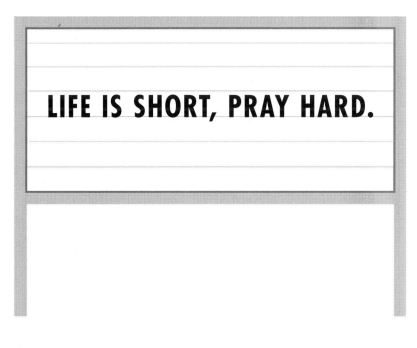

LIFE IS SHORT, PRAY HARD.

If you find yourself with time on your hands,
put 'em together and pray.

✦

Most often falling into sin is not a blowout
but a slow leak.

The Devil is not afraid of a dust-covered Bible.

◆

A big fall begins with a little stumble.

IT WASN'T THE APPLE ON THE TREE, IT WAS THE PAIR BENEATH.

The heaviest thing to carry is a grudge.

◆

God calls us to get into the game, not to keep score.

◆

When we've done what we can, God will do what we can't!

ine Easter heart, not the Easter hat.

◆

Pray hardest when it is hardest to pray.

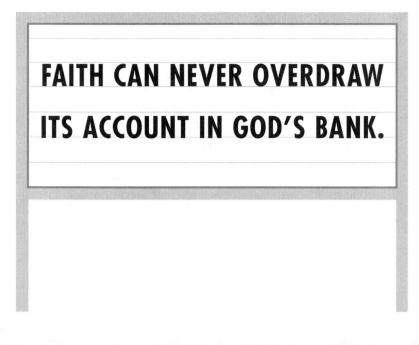

FAITH CAN NEVER OVERDRAW

ITS ACCOUNT IN GOD'S BANK.

Satan's greatest wile is "Wait a while."

♦

Tend your heart well—it is God's garden.

No burden is too heavy for the everlasting arms.

◆

Patience is a virtue that carries a lot of wait.

◆

I would never take *your* name in vain.
—God

Snap judgments have a way of
becoming unfastened.

✦

Not expecting answers from God wastes
His time and yours.

God may say "wait," but He never says "worry."

✦

Watch your step—everyone else does.

GOD'S RETIREMENT PLAN

IS OUT OF THIS WORLD.

Patience is counting down without blasting off.

✦

Beware: Two wrongs might make a riot.

✦

Sin won't keep you from the Bible, but the Bible can keep you from sin.

"Pray" is a four-letter word that you can say anywhere.

✦

For fast, fast relief, take two tablets.

EASTER — MORE

SOMETHING TO D

God judges us by direction, not by distance.

◆

Been taken for granted? I know how you feel.
—God

Ashes to ashes, dust to dust, in the Lord I do trust.

✦

God answers prayer with yes, no, or wait.

✦

JOY: Jesus first, Others second, Yourself last.

WHEN DOWN IN THE MOUTH,

REMEMBER JONAH.

HE CAME OUT ALL RIGHT.

Do you really want your children to grow up
to be just like you?

♦

A family altar can alter a family.

♦

Faith isn't a leap in the dark but a step into light.

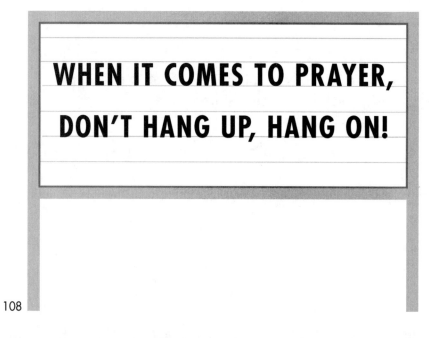

WHEN IT COMES TO PRAYER,
DON'T HANG UP, HANG ON!

To break sin's grip, put yourself in God's hands.

✦

Grace is everything—for nothing—to those
who don't deserve anything.

✦

Christians are not sinless, but they should sin less.

GOSSIP IS LIKE A BALLOON—IT GROWS BIGGER WITH EVERY PUFF.

Faith: Better to wear out than to rust out.

◆

Pessimists need a kick in the can'ts.

◆

Is what you're living for worth dying for?

The Easter story is not a dead issue.

✦

No one chills out in the fires of hell.

✦

Delay is preferable to error.

God gave us ten commandments,
not ten suggestions.

♦

Carve praise in stone; write criticism in sand.

♦

Don't stretch the truth—it may snap back at you.

You never have to explain something
you haven't said.

◆

You can't direct the wind, but you can
adjust your sails.

◆

Once wise men followed a star.
Now they follow the Son.

Christians, keep the faith—but not from others.

✦

Drive carefully. Your car isn't the only thing that can be recalled by its Maker.

✦

Let your resolution be His solution.

GOD DIDN'T TAKE THE TIME
TO CREATE A NOBODY.

117

Those who put God first will be happy at last.

✦

Shadows fall behind when we walk
toward the light.

✦

Life is like a game of hide-and-seek: We are all
either hiding from God or seeking Him.

The devil brings devastation—
God offers restoration.

◆

God's delays are not God's denials.

◆

Wanted: Sinners.

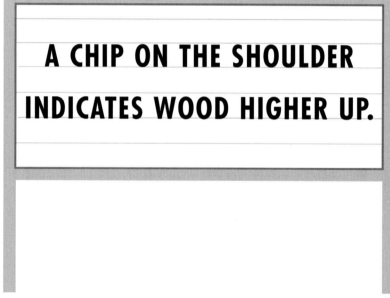

A CHIP ON THE SHOULDER INDICATES WOOD HIGHER UP.

120

ASAP—Always Say A Prayer.

◆

God's power comes to us when we
admit our powerlessness.

Preach the gospel at all times—
use words if necessary.

♦

Come worship in the Sonshine.

Breathe in God's spirit—exhale God's love.

✦

Sunny spirits make even the darkest skies shine.

✦

Fools rush in—and get all the best seats!

Smooth seas don't make skillful sailors.

✦

Christ crossed out our sins on Calvary.

✦

A good way to save face is to keep
the lower half closed.

You may need to lose everything to find that
God is all you need.

✦

Focus on a good life, not on a good living.

✦

We cannot enter heaven before heaven enters us.

THERE ARE TWO THINGS IN LIFE THAT I'VE LEARNED: THERE IS A GOD, AND I'M NOT HIM.

Move closer to God and He will move
closer to you.

◆

It takes only one candle to dispel darkness.

◆

If we depend on Christ for everything,
we can endure anything.

God is like Scotch tape: You can't see Him,
but you know He's there.

◆

Worry is interest paid on trouble before it is due.

◆

Only God is in a position to look down on anyone.

Swallowing angry words is always easier than eating them.

◆

The fruitful life seeks rain as well as sunshine.

CAN I RECOMMEND A GOOD BOOK FOR THIS SUMMER'S READING? — GOD

Christians are like coals of a fire. Together they glow—apart they grow cold.

✦

Everyone wants to harvest but few want to plow.

✦

The best vitamin for a Christian is B1.

He who has no money is poor. He who has nothing but money is even poorer.

✦

Earth is the only hell a Christian will ever know, but the only heaven a non-Christian will ever know.

People who walk with God always get
to their destination.

✦

Happiness is an inside job.

Mary Compton, a native of North Carolina, earned her Ph.D. at the University of Mississippi. She is a writer and editor.

David Compton, born in Atlanta, was a marketing executive with several *Fortune 500* companies before turning to writing. He is the national bestselling author of *Executive Sanction* and *Impaired Judgment*, and is currently at work on his next novel.